Giovanna Magi

JERUSALEM

110 Colour illustrations

BONECHI & STEIMATZKY

The Temple of Herod in the model of ▶ Jerusalem at the Holyland Hotel. The model, built on a scale of 1:50, depicts Jerusalem as it must have appeared in 66 A. D., the end of the Second Temple era, just before the Romans destroyed the Temple in 70 A. D. The model's construction was supervised by Prof. Michael Avi Yonah and was based on descriptions of the city given by Josephus Flavius, the Talmud and Mishna.

CONTENTS

© Copyright 1998 by CASA EDITRICE BONECHI - Via Cairoli 18/b - 50131 Florence - Italy - Tel. 55/576841 - Fax 55/5000766
E-mail: bonechi@bonechi.it - Internet: www.bonechi.it
Team work. All rights reserved. No part of this publication may be reproduced or transmitted in any form or by any means, electronic, chemical or mechanical, including photocopying, recording, or by any information storage and retrieval system, without permission in writing from the publisher. The cover, layout and artwork by the CASA EDITRICE BONECHI graphic artists in this publication are protected by international copyright.
Printed in Italy by Centro Stampa Editoriale Bonechi.
Translated by Claire Seminario
Photographs from the Archives of Casa Editrice Bonechi taken by:
Garo Nalbandian *and* Alessandro Saragosa

ISBN 88-7009-253-4

* * *

JERUSALEM

Condensing Jerusalem's four-thousand-year history into a few pages is difficult indeed, particularly since Jerusalem's past is so immensely varied and dramatic.

Situated in the Judean mountains, Jerusalem is a city sacred to humanity. For Moslems, it is El Kuds, the Holy; for Jews, Yerushalim, their capital city since the time of King David; for Christians, the site of Christ's Passion and Crucifixion. The name «Jerusalem» means «City of Peace», but how few have been the periods of peace in its history! Jerusalem has been invaded and laid waste by the Egyptians, Babylonians, Greeks, Romans, Persians, Moslems, Christians, Mamelukes and the Turks.

Jerusalem's first inhabitants lived on the hill south of the Temple Mount area which Josephus called the Ophel. They were a Canaanite tribe called the Jebusites. Their city had been mentioned in an Egyptian Execration Text of the second millennium B.C. as «Ursalim», one of a long list of cities conquered by Pharaoh. In 1000 B.C., David conquered Jerusalem and bought the top of Mount Moriah from the Jebusite king Arauna on which to build an altar to the Lord. He transferred the Ark of the Covenant, symbolizing the union between God and his people, there from Hebron.

It had accompanied the People of Israel throughout the long years of wandering in the desert before arriving in the Promised Land and had gone with them into many battles.

Solomon, son of David and Bathsheba, also chose Mount Moriah as the site for the grand and sumptuous First Temple he built around 950 B.C. The Temple itself was later destroyed but the wisdom of its builder would be remembered for centuries to come. After Solomon's death, discord among the tribes split his kingdom into two parts: Israel in the north and Judah, with its capital in Jerusalem, in the south. The kingdom of Israel succumbed to Assyrian advances shortly thereafter and became an Assyrian province. Judah resisted a bit longer. While King Sennacherib failed to conquer Jerusalem in 701 B.C., the Babylonian Nebuchadnezzar succeeded to do so in 587 B.C. He sacked the city, destroyed the Temple and took thousands of Jews back with him to Babylonia. This Babylonian exile lasted nearly fifty years, until the Persian King Cyrus conquered Babylonia and allowed the exiles to begin their return to Judah. Approximately one hundred years later, Nehemiah the Prophet and Ezra the Scribe supervised the

3

Panorama of Jerusalem from the Mount
of Olives. On the left, the site of the
Temple with the Dome of the Rock.

rebuilding of the Temple in Jerusalem as well as the walls
around the city, which were completed in record time.
With the arrival of Alexander the Great in 333 B.C., the
country saw the beginning of its «Hellenistic» era, when
Greek pagan ideas infiltrated the Jewish culture and led to
serious clashes. When Emperor Antiochus Epiphanes IV
declared himself divine and commanded the Jews to sacri-
fice pigs on their altars to him, the Maccabbean Revolt
ignited, culimating in the ousting of the Greeks (Seleu-
cids) from Jerusalem in 164 B.C. For the next century, the
Hasmonean dynasty of Jewish kings ruled the country. In
63 B.C. as Pompey led his legions into Jerusalem, the
Land (now composed of Judah, Samaria, the Galilee, the
Golan and the Negev) became part of the Roman Empire.
In 37 B.C., the Roman Senate gave the title of king to
Herod, who would later be known as Herod the Great.
Despite the resentment the population felt toward him,
Herod brought Jerusalem to unprecedented magnificence
by expanding and rebuilding the Temple and by his many
other monumental building projects in the city.

After his death in the year 4 B.C., his kingdom was
divided among his three sons. During the reign of one of
them, Herod Antipas, Jesus was crucified on orders of the
Procurator, Pontius Pilate, in Jerusalem.

The ever more frequent and bloody Jewish rebellions
against the heavy-handed Romans led to the destruction of
Herod's Temple by Titus in the year 70 A.D. Sixty years
later, another major revolt led by a Jew named Bar Kochba,
precipitated the complete leveling of the city of Jerusalem
by the Roman general Hadrian. On its ruins he erected the
pagan city of Aelia Capitolina and forbade Jews to set foot
there. At the same time, he changed the name of the
country to «Palestina». Most of the Jews were forced to
leave by famine, persecution and intolerably heavy taxes.
Thus began the great Dispersion of the Jewish people
throughout the world.

When the Roman Emperor Constantine embraced
Christianity in the early fourth century, the Byzantine Era
began. Jerusalem became a Christian city, with the Holy
Sepulcher its centerpiece. The Persians, under Cosroe II,
invaded the city, destroyed the Holy Sepulcher and depor-
ted much of the population in 614 A.D. Twenty-three
years later, Omar led the Moslem invasion of Jerusalem.
For the next four hundred years, Jerusalem took on the
complexion of Islam, and was called by the Moslems, «El
Kuds», «the Holy». According to the Koran, Abraham,
David and Solomon were also great prophets before Mo-
hammed. The tradition that Mohammed made his «Night
Journey» to heaven was associated with the Temple
Mount, where the Dome of the Rock and the Al-Aksa
Mosque were built in 691 and 703 A.D., respectively.

In 1099, the Crusaders arrived from Europe to liberate

Christian holy sites from the «infidels». They conquered Jerusalem and immediately set about rebuilding their holiest shrine, the Holy Sepulcher. Jerusalem became a city of churches and monasteries until 1187, when the Moslem leader Saladin recaptured it. The city was to come into Christian hands once again before the Crusaders were summarily ousted from the country by the Mamelukes at the end of the thirteenth century. Jerusalem sank into a dusty, poverty-stricken stupor, its population dwindling to a mere 11,000 by mid-nineteenth century.

Following the Crimean War, interest in the Holy Land was rekindled. The first Jewish neighbourhoods began to crop up around the walled city in the 1860's, and by 1915, the Jewish population of the city had swelled to 100,000.

On December 9, 1917, the British General Allenby accepted the surrender of the city of Jerusalem from the Turks and three years later, the British Mandate of Palestine began. Finding the Jewish-Arab rivalry in Palestine too great a burden, England relinquished its Mandate in 1947. On November 29 of that year, the United Nations voted to partition the Mandate between the Jews and the Arabs of Palestine. Within hours the newborn Jewish state was attacked by its Arab neighbours on all sides, a conflict which was to become known as the Independence War of 1948. A year and a half later, ceasefire lines were drawn, placing Jerusalem's Old City with all its holy sites in Jordan and the newer, western side of the city in Israel. A wall was built through the heart of Jerusalem, cutting off the population of each side from the other for nineteen years.

On June 5, 1967, Jordanian artillery opened fire on the Jewish side of the city. It was a thoughtless act that within 48 hours brought about the reunification of the city under Jewish control. On June 27, the State of Israel annexed the Old City and tore down the wall which had divided east from west. It was as though a dam had burst; people flooded from each side of the city to the other, some seeing the opposite end for the first time ever. Amid tremendous excitement, intermingling and reunions took place. However, once inside the Old City, the Jews made the painful discovery that the Jordanians had blown up the twenty-seven synagogues and many of the religious schools there. Those which hadn't been destroyed had been used as latrines, stables and garbage heaps. But the Wall, the Wailing Wall, had survived the vandalism. Its environs were cleared and thousands of Jews poured into the Old City to touch and kiss its ancient stones for the first time in two thousand years. It now became known as the Western Wall because it would attract all people not just in sorrow, as in the past, but in joy as well. The long exile was over. Returned to their city, Jews rebuilt her synagogues and houses, lanes and public squares with loving tenderness. Throughout two thousand years of separation from Jerusalem, Jews have repeated each day, «Next Year in Jerusalem!» Today, their hopes of returning to Zion have been realized.

5

Menorah - The seven-branched candlelabrum («menorah») has been the symbol of the Jewish people since ancient times. This giant bronze menorah, on which there appear twenty-nine scenes from Jewish history sculpted in bas-relief, was done by Benno Elkan and presented as a gift from the British Parliament to the State of Israel in 1956. It is inscribed with the words: «The Menorah is a symbol of the light of faith and hope which has led the Jewish people for four thousand years often through martyrdom in their mission of upholding the religion of righteousness among men and between nations. It is the emblem of the State of Israel. This menorah commemorating the great personages and events of Jewish history is presented to the Knesset as a gift from Britain. 1956».

The windmill - In the mid-19th century, when conditions inside Jerusalem's Jewish quarter became unbearably crowded, philanthropists Sir Moses Montefiori and Yehuda Touro built new housing outside the city's walls. Jews who were courageous enough to venture outside what is now called «The Old City» were accommodated there. Montefiori built the windmill on the hill above this new housing complex for the residents to mill their own flour. It never functioned, however, because it was relatively too low on the landscape. Still, it is one of Jerusalem's most familiar landmarks.

Ramot - At the end of the Six Day War in 1967, the walls and barbed wire fences which had cut Jerusalem in half were taken down. The previously divided Jewish and Arab sections spilled into one another and the city was reunited. In the early 1970's, several new neighbourhoods were constructed around Jerusalem as a «security belt»: Ramot, Neveh Yaacov, Pisgat Zeev and Givat Zeev to the north, Talpiot Mizrach and Gilo to the southeast.

Jaffa Road - Named Jaffa Road because it begins at Jaffa Gate and leads the traveler in the direction of the port of Jaffa on the Mediterranean coast, this busy street in the heart of Jerusalem's shopping district is a must for every visitor.

The new neighbourhood of Ramot in northern Jerusalem. ▶

Early morning on Jaffa Road, one of Jerusalem's main ▶
streets.

The Menorah which stands outside Israel's parliament, the Knesset.

The windmill, one of Jerusalem's most familiar landmarks.

The Damascus Gate, with its festive animation.

From left to right and top to bottom: ▶
Herod's Gate, the Lion's Gate, the
Golden Gate and the Zion Gate.

The Walls and Gates - Jerusalem's Old City is surrounded by a splendid two and a half mile limestone wall built by the Turkish ruler, Suleiman the Magnificent, between 1536 and 1539. The walls have seven gates. The most beautiful is the **Damascus Gate**, with its many turrets. Recent excavations have revealed the ancient Roman entrance beneath it. **Herod's Gate** or the Flower Gate, leads the visitor into the Moslem Quarter of the city. Towards the Mount of Olives is the **Lions Gate**, called St. Stephen's Gate by the Christians who believe that the saint was martyred there. The Arabs call it Bab Sittia Maryan (The Virgin Mary's Gate) because her birthplace is thought to be inside this gate. The **Golden Gate**, or **Mercy Gate**, is divided into two arches which were blocked up by the Moslems. Tradition has it that Jesus passed through here on his way to the Temple. It is also believed that the gate was built by the Byzantines over foundations laid by King Solomon. The **Dung Gate**, named thus because the city's Christian inhabitants threw their garbage on the ruins of the Temple Mount in Byzantine times, leads the visitor directly into the Western Wall area. The **Zion Gate**, which gives access to the Jewish Quarter, is called by the Arabs Bab el Daoud (David) because it faces Mount Zion, the traditional burial place of King David. The **Jaffa Gate**, one of the city's busiest gates, stands at the beginning of Jaffa Road, leading west to the coast and port of Jaffa. Called Bab el Khalil in Arabic, the gate was opened and a road paved through it in 1898 to allow Kaiser Wilhelm's carriage to pass through. The **New Gate** was opened in 1889.

The Jaffa Gate.

The Tower of David, with its characteristic minarets.

The Citadel and Tower of David - Situated next to Jaffa Gate, the Citadel encompasses an area where once stood three towers built by King Herod: the Phasael Tower (named for his brother), Hippicus Tower (names for his friend) and the Miriamne Tower (named for his wife). They were to guard Herod's adjacent palace and were later spared destruction by Titus' Roman army in order to house his Twelfth Legion. During the Byzantine era, it was in such a state of ruin that philosophers and recluses chose it as a place of meditation. It was used as a fortress headquarters in the 12th century by the Crusaders, who repaired its walls and surrounded it by a moat. The Moslem Mamelukes demolished it in 1239 and it remained in a state of abandon until 1335 when the Turks repaired its walls and added the minaret known today as the **Tower of David**. The Citadel became a British base during the Mandate (1917-1948) and then a Jordanian one until 1967. Today, it houses several museums and is famous for the sound and light shows presented on its walls.

The suggestive spectacle of sound and light in the citadel.

Arch of the Hurva Synagogue and the
façade of the Tiferet Israel Synagogue.

◀ The reconstruction of the ancient north-south road.

◀ The Cardo: one aspect
of the recently restored Jewish quarter.

The Jewish Quarter - Devoid of Jews between the reign
of Emperor Hadrian and the end of the Crusades, the
Jewish Quarter was populated by rabbis and their
students between the 13th century and the 1948 Independence War. It was taken by the Jordanian Legion and
almost completely leveled by the time of the Six Day War
in 1967. Since then, the Jewish Quarter has been
undergoing careful archaeological examination and restoration, and its homes and streets have been rebuilt. The
Hurva Synagogue, blown up in 1948, had been built in
1740 on the remains of a 13th century synagogue and it is
recognizable by its single restored arch. The **Tiferet Israel
Synagogue**, its name meaning «glory of Israel», was one
of the last pockets of resistance before the quarter fell in
1948. It can be identified by its three arched entrances.

Wilson Arch - Located to the left of the Western (or Wailing) Wall, this arch was named for Charles Wilson who discovered it in 1865. Beneath this medieval structure lies the original Herodian arch which supported the bridge connecting Second Temple Jerusalem's Upper City with the Temple Mount. Ongoing excavations have revealed another seventeen courses of the beautifully dressed Herodian stone beneath the present floor level.

The Broad Wall - Discovered during excavations in the Jewish Quarter immediately after the Six Day War, this seven meter wide stone wall was part of the fortification King Hezekiah built to encompass his city in 701 B. C. Many refugees from the northern tribes of Israel had come to Jerusalem for protection from the Assyrians who threatened the north. They settled to the west and were included in the city when this wall was completed.

Herodian Quarter - Beneath the imposing Wohl Torah Study Center are the remains of several mansions dating from the Herodian Dynasty period (37 B. C.-70 A. D.). The lower floors preserved here are especially rich, with many colorful mosaics and frescoes, and are full of bath tubs, ritual bath pools (mikvehs) and cisterns. These mansions belonged to the aristocracy of the Second Temple Period, the Sadducees, who were the priests and Temple administrators.

◄ *Jews in prayer at the Wilson Arch.*

◄ *View of the Wailing Wall.*

*General view of the Wailing Wall
dominated by the dome of the Omar mosque.*

WESTERN (WAILING) WALL

Symbol of Jewish faith and object of Jewish pilgrimage from all over the world, the Western Wall (Hakotel Hama'aravi) is a remnant of the western retaining wall of Herod's Temple Mount. It acquired the name «Wailing Wall» because during the long exile of the Jewish people from the city, they could return only once a year to mourn the destruction of the Temple. Throughout nearly two thousand years of exile, Jews from all parts of the world turned their faces in prayer toward this Wall in the hope of return. The Wall became the symbol of reconquest of the

city and reunification of the Jewish State when, in June of 1967, the first Israeli soldiers reached it. It was an unforgettably emotional event in the history of the Jewish people. Today, there is always someone praying at the Western Wall, whether throngs of people gathered for the holidays or just a few lingerers in the middle of the night.

One well-known custom associated with the Wall is to insert small papers on which are written prayers into the fissures between the monumental Herodian stones.

15

Jewish tourists insert their prayers to God between the Wall's bricks.

Two moments of the Bar Mitzvah: this ceremony takes place when male children reach their thirteenth birthday. The great Sefer Torah in painted wood guards the book of laws.

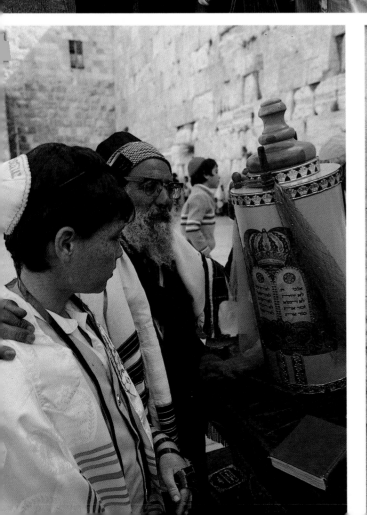

The recent excavations under the site of
the Temple. To the right, the silver dome
of the Al Aqsa Mosque.

Dung Gate.

The Dung Gate - The Dung Gate, on the southern wall
of Jerusalem's Old City, leads the visitor into the Western
Wall Plaza. It received this name during the Byzantine era
when the city's residents threw their garbage here in the
area of the Temple Mount.

The Al-Aqsa-Mosque - The Al Aqsa Mosque can be
identified by its black dome and its arched, Romanesque
facade. Its name means «the farthest away», referring to
the place farthest from Mecca and Medina that the
Prophet would reach on his Night Journey. The modest
mosque built by Walid in 709 was later greatly enlarged
by the Templar Crusaders who entered the city in 1099.
They named their new basilica «Templum Solomonis».
With the ousting of the Crusaders from the country by the
Mamelukes in the late 13th century, the entire structure
became the Al Aqsa Mosque. It suffered considerable

◀ *Exterior and interior of the El Aqsa Mosque.*

On this and the following page, the crowd in the Mosque of Omar during the Ramadan.

damage due to earthquakes but underwent massive restoration between 1938 and 1943. During this time, the marble columns (a gift of Mussolini) and the ceiling (given by the then Egyptian king Farouk), were added. The mosque has witnessed two recent dramatic events. On July 20, 1951, Jordan's King Abdullah was assassinated at the door. Today's King Hussein, who was with him, was miraculously saved by the heavy decorations he was wearing on his chest. Traces of the flying bullets are still visible on a column there. The other event occurred in 1969 when a crazed Australian set a fire inside the mosque causing damage that is still being repaired today.

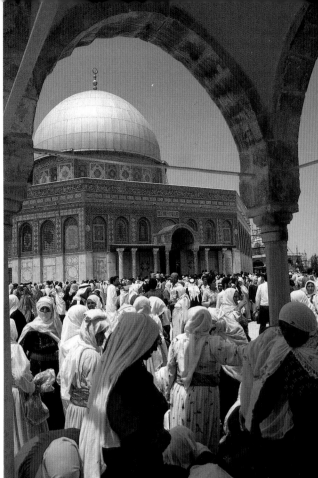

Detail of the sacred rock inside the ►
Mosque of Omar.

THE TEMPLE SITE AND DOME OF THE ROCK

The gate through which one ascends the Temple Mount from the Western Wall area is called the Mughrabi Gate, recalling the North Africa Moslems whose homes once clustered nearby.

The Haram es Sharif, or «The Nobel Sanctuary», covers about thirty acres in the shape of a trapezoid. It is sacred to the Moslems as the third place of pilgrimage after Mecca and Medina. It is sacred to the Jews as the site where Abraham nearly sacrificed his son, Isaac. Here stood Solomon's Temple, of which no trace remains, but which was meticulously described in the Books of Ezekiel and Kings. The Temple, resplendent with its carved cedarwood panels and gold-plated rosettes, housed the Ark of the Covenant which held the Ten Commandments,

the «covenant» between God and the Jewish people. Only the High Priest could enter the Holy of Holies where the Ark was kept, and then only on the Day of Atonement (Yom Kippur). The Temple was destroyed by Nebuchadnezzar in 587 B. C. and the Ark was lost. What is visible today are actually remains of the Second Temple, built by Herod the Great around 20 B. C. Its enormous foundations were supported by four retaining walls and many internal arches known today as Solomon's Stables. When the Moslems arrived there in 638 A. D., they found the Temple Mount had been covered with refuse. They cleared it and reinstated it as a place of worship since, according to Moslem tradition, Mohammed made his ascent into heaven (Night Journey) from here. In 687

The so-called Stables of King Solomon:
here the Crusaders kept their horses and camels.

A.D., Ommayad caliph Abd el Malik decided to erect a mosque on the spot and entrusted the job to Christian-Byzantine architects. Perched on an embankment accessible by flights of steps on four sides, the splendid **Dome of the Rock** (sometimes called the **Mosque of Omar**) presides over the entire Temple Mount area. Octagonal in form, it consists of a high base of colored marble, a 16th century reconstruction of the original model, from which rises the round drum covered with arabesque tiles of azure blue majolica. This beautiful ceramic decoration is thanks to Suleiman the Magnificent, who in 1552, had the famous Persian factories of Kashan fire this majolica to replace the previous mosaic walls of the mosque. It is crowned by the gold-colored dome, which was originally lead. Inside, the prayers and praises of Allah visible on the frieze were done in 1876 by the famous Turkish calligrapher, Mohammed Chafik. The interior of the mosque, with its double rows of 12 pillars and 28 monolithic columns is illuminated by 36 stained-glass windows. A carved wood screen encircles the bare bedrock in the center. A few steps lead to the grotto beneath the rock known to the Moslems as the «cave of the spirits». It is believed that the souls of pious Moslems gather here on Thursday evenings just before the Moslem Sabbath, Friday.

The exterior of the Church of St. Anne and, next to it, the excavations where the pool of Bathsheba or Probatical Pool, with its two pools and five doorways, was found. Here, Jesus cured the paraplegic.

The church's crypt.

Church of St. Anne - A true gem of Crusader architecture, the church of St. Anne is one of Jerusalem's best preserved medieval structures. This church of austere, simple beauty, maintained by the White Fathers since 1878, was built in the place to which tradition assigns the birth of Mary. Her parents, Anne and Joachim, had their home here. It was built in 1142 at the request of Queen Arda, widow of Baldwin I of Jerusalem, who had retired to a nearby convent. The interior has three naves with elegantly capitalled columns on top of which are vaulted arches. In the crypt opening below, a Baroque altar commemorates the birth of Mary.

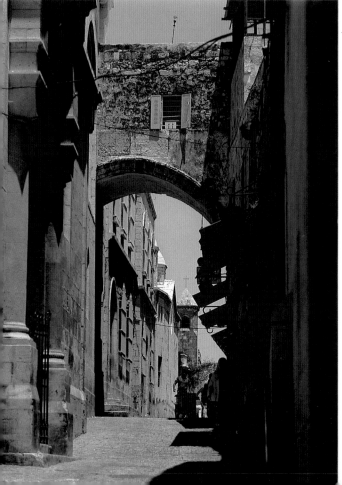

THE VIA DOLOROSA

Legend has it that almost immediately after the crucifixion of Jesus, his followers began to retrace his steps to Calvary. The term «Via Dolorosa» («The Way of Sorrows») was popularized in the 16th century and its fourteen stations were standardized by the Franciscans during the 19th century. This route, followed by the world's orthodox Christians, led from the Antonia Fortress, where Jesus appeared before Pilate and was condemned, out to Calvary (called Golgotha in Greek), which was outside the city walls at that time. (Alternate site: The Garden Tomb. See below).

First Station - The Chapel of the Flagellation where tradition holds that Jesus was interrogated by Pilate. The Franciscans begin their weekly procession through the Stations of the Cross here, on Friday afternoons. This modest chapel was built on the site of a Crusader oratory. Inside are glass panels representing the scourging of Jesus (center), Pilate cleansing his hands of the «blood of the innocent» (left), and the liberation of Barabas (right). On the dome above the altar is a large crown of golden thorns perforated by stars.

Ecce Homo Arch - This is the second station along the Via Dolorosa. In the 16th century, pilgrims began to refer to the arch as the Ecce Homo Arch, referring to Pilate's

declaration as he presented Jesus to the crowd of spectators, «Behold the man!». In reality it is part of a triumphal arch built by Hadrian in 135 A. D. to commemorate his conquest of Jerusalem. The original arch had three parts: the largest, central arch which spans the Via Dolorosa, the left arch which is no longer in existence, and the right arch that can still be seen today inside the Church of the Sisters of Zion.

The Struthion Pools - One of the Struthion Pools, originally built during the reign of the Hasmonean king Hyrcanus I (2nd century BC), it was partially destroyed by Herod when he built a moat around his Antonia Fortress and was later given a vaulted ceiling by Hadrian (135 A.D.).

Church of the Sisters of Zion - Here in this church are the remains of an ancient Roman pavement, the «Lithostratos». Drawings for dice games can still be seen etched in some of the slabs. Christian tradition has it that Roman soldiers played dice for Jesus' garments, and dice similar to those depicted in the drawings have actually been found.

Third Station - A small chapel built by Polish Catholic cavalrymen marks the spot where Jesus fell for the first time. The chapel belongs to the Armenian Catholic Patriarchate.

Fourth Station - A bas-relief sculpture by Zieliensky indicates the place where Jesus met his mother.

Fifth Station - As the inscription above the door of this Franciscan chapel says, here Simon of Cyrene took the cross from Jesus and carried it on to Golgotha. This is mentioned in three Gospels, but not in that of John.

Sixth Station - The Armenian Orthodox church here recalls Veronica who wiped the brow of Jesus with her veil. The impression of His face remained on the veil which has been kept in St. Peter's since 707. Inside the church is the tomb of St. Veronica.

Seventh Station - Here the Via Dolorosa intersects the noisy bazaar, and a column marked with the Roman numerals VII indicates where Jesus fell for the second time.

Eighth Station - A small plaque with a cross on the wall marks the place where Jesus met the pious women of Jerusalem and told them, «Don't weep for me, daughters of Jerusalem, but for yourselves and your children.»

Ninth Station - A column near the Ethiopian monastery shows the place where Jesus fell for the third time. The last five stations of the Via Dolorosa are inside the Holy Sepulchre.

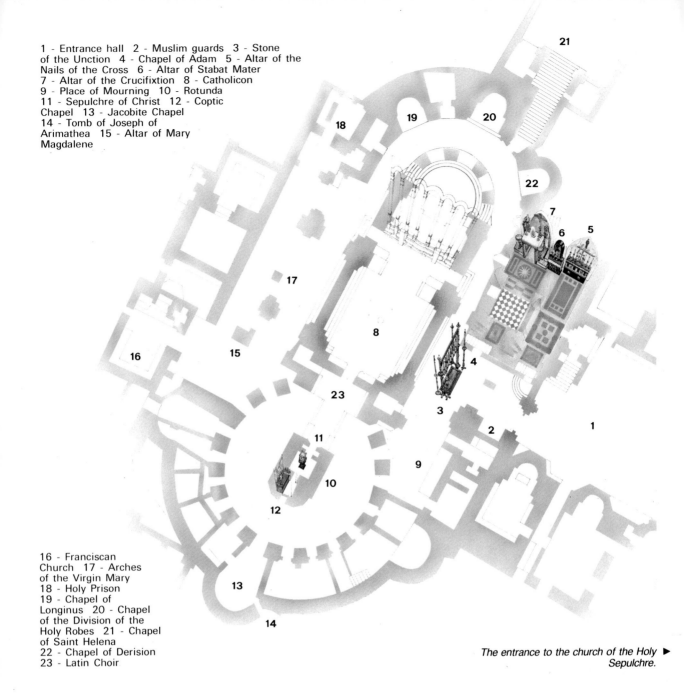

1 - Entrance hall 2 - Muslim guards 3 - Stone of the Unction 4 - Chapel of Adam 5 - Altar of the Nails of the Cross 6 - Altar of Stabat Mater 7 - Altar of the Crucifixtion 8 - Catholicon 9 - Place of Mourning 10 - Rotunda 11 - Sepulchre of Christ 12 - Coptic Chapel 13 - Jacobite Chapel 14 - Tomb of Joseph of Arimathea 15 - Altar of Mary Magdalene

16 - Franciscan Church 17 - Arches of the Virgin Mary 18 - Holy Prison 19 - Chapel of Longinus 20 - Chapel of the Division of the Holy Robes 21 - Chapel of Saint Helena 22 - Chapel of Derision 23 - Latin Choir

*The entrance to the church of the Holy ►
Sepulchre.*

THE HOLY SEPULCHRE

The Church of the Holy Sepulchre is the most sacred site to Orthodox Christianity in Jerusalem. The quarry here was once an execution grounds outside the city's gates, with a hill plainly visible to everyone travelling to or from the city. It was called Golgotha, from the Hebrew word «golgolet», or «skull», which is what the hill resembled. In addition, there is a legend that Adam was buried here. Near Golgotha were many stone tombs which had been hewn into the surrounding bedrock. The area was incorporated by the Emperor Hadrian into his new city, Aelia Capitolina, as a Forum and Temple area, dedicated to Jupiter, Juno and Venus. Hadrian built this new pagan city over the ruins of Jerusalem, which he had completely destroyed in retaliation for a major Jewish revolt. (It was also at this time that he changed the name of the country from Israel/Judea to Palestine.)

Fortunately, Hadrian didn't level the rocks into which the tombs were dug for the construction of his Capitoline Temple. Instead, he limited himself to filling those spaces and leveling them off by placing large quantities of earth

The altar of the Nails of the Cross, on Golgotha.

*To the right, the small altar called Stabat ▶
Mater, and next to it, that of the
Crucifixtion, with the life size icons of
Christ, the Virgin and John.*

around' them. By doing so, he created a base for the temple, an enormous terrace that preserved the tombs from destruction.

In 331 A. D., the mother of Constantine the Great, Helena, and Bishop Macarius, travelled to the Holy Land to find Jesus' birthplace, tomb and other places important to Christianity. The excavations that the empress carried out here revealed the tomb of Jesus, His cross and those of the two thieves. Constantine had all the rocks and earth removed to expose Golgotha, where he placed a cross covered by a tabernacle, and the tomb, which he enclosed in a hugh rotunda called the «Anastasis», meaning Resurrection. The work was completed in 335 A. D. The basilica which stood east of the rotunda was destroyed by the Persians in 614. Reconstruction began 15 years later under the abbot Modestus and the church remained intact until the caliph El-Hakim had it totally razed in 1009.

When the Crusaders entered the city on July 15, 1099, they found the church as it had been reconstructed by the Emperor Constantine Monomachus. As it did not seem suitable to them, they took on the task of rebuilding the church almost entirely. The new edifice was completed in 1149. A ferocious fire devastated much of the church in 1808, but the western world, preoccupied with Napoleon in Europe, virtually ignored pleas for assistance in reconstructing it. The Greek Orthodox assumed control of the church and its repair, hence its present, predominantly eastern character.

Today, the inside of the Holy Sepulchre is divided among five communities: Roman Catholic, Greek Orthodox and Armenian (who together control most of the church), Copts and Syrian Orthodox. The Ethiopian monks have their cells and chapel on the roof of the church.

Golgotha - The Golgotha of today, accessible by steep steps, has two chapels side by side, one Roman Catholic and the other Greek Orthodox. On the Roman side are two Stations: where Jesus was stripped of his garments and where he was nailed to the cross. On the Greek side, the 12th Station: where Jesus died on the cross. Under the altar can be seen the top of the rocky outcrop with a silver marker where it is believed the cross stood. In between the two is the Stabat Mater, («Sorrowful Mother») in remembrance of Mary's agony at her son's death.

The Annointing Stone - Here tradition has it that Jesus was laid when he was taken down from the cross. His body was sprinkled with a mixture of myrrh and aloe and he was mourned by his mother before being laid in the tomb. This is the 13th Station of the Cross.

The Tomb - The edicule, the artificial structure that stands in the center of the anastasis, simulates the original two-roomed tomb of hewn stone. One enters the first room, the *Chapel of the Angel*, where a richly ornamented cube of marble is encased. It is believed to have been part of the tomb cover on which the angel was seated when the women came to annoint Jesus' body on Sunday morning and found the tomb empty. The second room is the mortuary chamber and the last station of the Via Dolorosa. A white marble slab about two yards long covers the bathtub type tomb which had been donated by Joseph of Arimathea. Above the tomb are 43 hanging lamps: four belonging to the Copts and the others equally divided among the Latins, Greeks and Armenians. An icon of the Virgin conceals part of the primitive rock tomb.

General view of the entrance to the Holy Sepulchre, with the Stone of the Unction in the foreground.

General view of the tomb of Christ.

The small space preserving the ▶ tombstone of the tomb of Christ.

Katholikoṅ - This is the main body of the basilica, containing the inconostasis, the heavily decorated partition which separates the altar from the rest of the congregation. The large omphalos dome rises above the transept; it marks what many Christians consider to be «the center of the world».

Holy Prison - This narrow space, known also as the Prison of Christ, is really an ancient jail annexed to the Aelia Capitolina. Tradition identifies it as the jail in which Jesus spent the night after his arrest in Gethsemane.

Chapel of Saint Helena - This lower level chapel is dedicated to the mother of Constantine. It was built by the Crusaders and still rests on four 11th century columns. The chapel belongs to the Armenians.

Tomb of Joseph of Arimathea - This is the only part of the Holy Sepulchre belonging to the Ethiopian community. It is a small, rock-hewn tomb in the wall of the rotunda. Joseph of Arimathea, a wealthy member of the Sanhedrin, owned the tomb into which Jesus was laid, and was called «a good and just man who was waiting for the reign of God».

The iconostasis in the Katholikon and the dome over the crossing seen from below.

The interior of Christ's prison.

The rock excavated form the Tomb of Joseph of Arimathea.

The beautiful crypt of St. Helena.

Church of Saint Mark - A 7th century chapel already existed on this spot, which was then restored by the Crusaders. The actual 19th century church of Syrian-Orthodox denomination is part of the Jacobite convent.

Church of Saint James - This is an Armenian-Orthodox church of which the actual state is due to the renovation of an 11th century construction. It was built in memory of the martyrdom of James the Great, brother of the evangelist John: James was beheaded here in 44 A.D. under orders of Herod the Great and ruler of Palestine from 41 to 44. His persecution of the Christians was dictated by the fact that he wanted to earn the position of priest. The richly ornamented interior conserves stones from sacred locations in the history of Israel: the Sinai, the Tabor, and the Jordan.

Church of Saint John the Baptist - The domes and bell towers of Jerusalem soar up against the blue skies and over the rooftops of Jerusalem. The one dedicated to John the Baptist, of Greek-Orthodox denomination, was built in the 11th century above a crypt.

Church of St. Mary Magdalene - Easily identifiable by its brilliant, onion-shaped gold domes, this White Russian Orthodox church was built between 1885 and 1888 by the Czar Alexander III in memory of his mother, Mary Alexandrova. Inside are many beautiful icons and the tomb of the Grand Duchess Elizabeth Feodorovna, who was assassinated in 1918.

Exterior and interior of the Church of St. Mark.

Exterior of the Church of St. James. ▶

The domes of the Russian Church of St. Mary ▶
Magdalene.

The bell-tower of the Church of St. John ▶
the Baptist amidst the roofs of Jerusalem.

Market - The streets of Jerusalem are full of twists and turns. Here one can buy anything because the market sells everything: colorful Arab clothing and headdresses, olive wood carvings, pieces of antique amber, perfumed spices and religious articles.

City of David - Just outside the Dung Gate of the Old City is the village of Silwan (Siloam). It covers the hillside (called in the Bible «Ophel») down to the Kidron Valley. This is where Jerusalem originated five thousand years ago. The well-marked excavations of Area G show the visitor many levels of the ancient city, from the Canaanite, through the Israelite up to the Hasmonean period. One follows the path down to the Warren's Shaft, where one actually enters the three-thousand year old Jebusite tunnel leading to a vertical shaft through which the ancient dwellers drew their water in times of siege. At the bottom of the hill, in the Kidron Valley itself, is the famous **Gihon Spring** where Solomon was crowned king. Here is the entrance to **Hezekiah's Tunnel**, an incredible feat of engineering which channeled the waters of the Gihon through the rock under the City of David into the Pool of Siloam where they were accessible to the city's inhabitants. The Tunnel was built by King Hezekiah in 701 B.C. An ancient Hebrew inscription found here (and removed to Istambul by the Turks) described the momentous project of digging the tunnel.

Two typical streets of Jerusalem's market, in the old city.

The Valley of the Kidron.
On the left is the pillar of Absalom,
the tomb of James and the tomb of Zacharias.
The so-called Pillar of Absalom (Right).

Kidron Valley - Just one look at the Valley of Kidron from the top of the Mount of Olives is sufficient to understand why this place has impressed the population of Jerusalem since ancient times. The harshness of the landscape, the scarce vegetation, the graves dug into the bedrock or isolated among the olive trees give this place an air of timelessness. Popular belief says that here, the Final Resurrection and Final Judgement will take place. One version says that a fine wire will be strung from the Old City wall across the valley to the Mount of Olives, and everyone must walk across. The good will make it to the end and the sinners will fall off into the valley.

Three monumental tombs on the valley floor catch the eye. One is the **Pillar of Absalom**, the rebellious son of David who, «had this monument built while he was still alive, saying: 'Not having sons, this will be the record of my name' and he named it after himself, and today it is still called the Hand of Absalom» (Kings II, 18:18). This monument has a Greek-style conical top which is called a «ptolos». Near it is the tomb of Zacharia (or St. James) with a pyramidal top, and in between is the catacomb tomb of the Ben Hasir family. All three date back to the Hellenistic period.

The hill dotted with olive trees that
descend below the site of the Temple.

Exterior of the Church of the Tomb of Mary.

Church of the Tomb of Mary - The church's spare
lines go back to the age of the Crusaders (11th century)
and is of Greek-Orthodox denomination. Its interior
houses the tombs of Anna and Joachim, parents of Mary
and that of her husband Joseph as well. The rock-tomb
of the Virgin is found in a crypt, enriched with icons,
precious lamps and paintings.

The tombstone has three large holes in it permitting
worshippers to touch the inside of Mary's tomb. It
should not be forgotten however, that another tomb of
the Virgin exists at Ephesus in Turkey: in fact, according
to another version of the story, the apostle John took the
mother of Jesus with him to Ephesus, where she remained
until her death.

Gethsemane: the Church of all Nations and above, the Church of St. Mary Magdalene.

In the garden near the Church of all Nations are olive trees so old and contorted that they are considered to be direct descendants (if not the actual trees) of those that grew here in Jesus' time.

Views of the facade;
the mosaic on the main
altar with the rock, and
a detail of the crown of thorns.

The tunnel of the Pool of Siloah.

A detail of Gihon Spring.

Gethsemane - Church of All Nations - The name is derived from the Hebrew term for olive press, «gat shemen». Jesus endured his agony in the garden here before he was arrested. A sanctuary was built on the spot in the 4th century and later enlarged by the Crusaders. The present church, with its large, luminous mosaic in the tympanum, was built by the Italian Antonio Barluzzi between 1919 and 1924 on the remains of the previous structures. Inside, on the ceiling are the crests of nations who contributed to the church's construction. On the floor in front of the chalice-shaped altar is a crown of hammered steel thorns encircling a piece of rock where Jesus is believed to have knelt in prayer. The mosaic over the altar represents «_Christ in Agony_», those in the lateral apses are titled «_The Kiss of Judas_» and «_Christ's Arrest_».

Pool of Siloah - The pool of Siloah or Siloam, nestled at the lower end of the Tyropean Valley at the end of Hezekiah's Tunnel, holds the memory of Jesus' healing of the blind man, «Go bathe in the pool of Siloah» (John 9:7).

The Gihon Spring - Approach to the Gihon Spring. This was Jerusalem's primary water source in ancient times. When the Assyrians threatened the city, Judean king Hezekiah built his famous tunnel (701 B. C.) to convey water from the spring to the Siloam Pool, safe within the city walls.

The inscription on the stone reads:

THEN TOOK THEY THE ... THE TOMB, AND WOUND IT IN LINEN
CLOTHES WITH THE SPICES, AS THE MANNER OF THE JEWS IS TO BURY
NOW IN THE PLACE WHERE HE WAS CRUCIFIED THERE WAS A GARDEN
AND IN THE GARDEN A NEW SEPULCHRE, WHEREIN WAS NEVER MAN
YET LAID.
THERE LAID THEY JESUS THEREFORE BECAUSE OF THE
JEWS' PREPARATION DAY, FOR THE SEPULCHRE WAS NIGH
AT HAND.
John 19: 40-42

TO MNHMEION
ELABON OYN TO SOMA TOY IHSOY KAI EDHSAN AYTO OONIOIS
META TON AROMATON KAOOS ESOS HN TOIS IOYDAIOIS ENTAPHIAZEIN
HN DE EN TO TOPO OPOY ESTAYROOOH KHPOS KAI EN TO KHPO
MNHMEION KAINON, EN O OYDEPO OYDEIS KALEIS ... ETEOH.
EKEI OYN DIA THN PARASKEYHN TON IOYDAION, OTI EGGYS
HN TO MNHMEION, EOHKAN TON IHSOYN.
Ioannou 19: 40-42

The splendid panorama of Jerusalem as
enjoyed from the window of the Dominus Flevit.

The rock-hewn tomb.

◄ Gardens and walls at the Garden Tomb.

Church of Dominus Flevit - Here Jesus, nearing Jerusalem, stopped and wept over the destiny that awaited the city: «...and they won't leave you a stone standing because you haven't acknowledged the moment in which you have been visited».

The present church belongs to the Franciscans and was built by Barluzzi in the late 1930's over the ruins of a 5th century church. Remains of an ancient necropolis were discovered in the area, revealing numerous Hebrew, Aramic and Greek epitaphs. Absolutely unforgettable is the view of Jerusalem from the window over the altar.

Garden Tomb - Often called «Gordon's Calvary» after the British officer who first saw the site from the top of Damascus Gate, this rocky outcrop and garden around it contain an ancient tomb which many Christians believe to have been the sepulchre of Jesus. From many angles, the hill resembles a skull, and there are various other features about the garden (e.g., large cistern, wine press, location near city gate) which make it a plausible alternate site to the Holy Sepulchre. Its serene atmosphere and lovely gardens are, for many, much more conducive to prayer and contemplation. Free guided tours are conducted on request. The Garden Tomb is administered by the Garden Tomb Association founded and based in England.

Exterior and interior of the tomb of Lazarus.

On the next page, the chapel of the ▶
Ascension and the Church of St. Peter in Gallicantu.

Tomb of Lazarus - It is written in the Gospel of St. John: «There was an ill man, a certain Lazarus of Bethany, the village of Mary and Martha, his sister... Bethany was about fifteen furlongs from Jerusalem».

Today the village of Bethany is called Azariyeh in Arabic, after the ancient Lazarion of Byzantine times. Lazarus' tomb, today property of the Moslems, is reached by descending 24 steep steps put there in the 17th century. Here, the body of Lazarus was resuscitated by the words of Jesus.

Church of the Ascension - According to the Gospels, Jesus reappeared to the apostles forty days after the Resurrection and took them to the top of the Mount of Olives and «...while he blessed them, he separated himself from them and ascended up into Heaven». Here then, the earthly life of Christ was concluded. The supernatural event is remembered here by a 13th century chapel belonging to the Moslems for whom, it must be remembered, Jesus was one of the great prophets.

This chapel originally had a double, circular portico and open arcades. Now the small round building houses the rock with a footprint said to be that of Jesus from the moment of his ascension.

Church of Saint Peter in Gallicantu - The name given to this church records the episode in which Peter denied the Master three times after the crow of the rooster. The actual church, consecrated in 1931 and belonging to the Assumptionists of Catholic denomination, rises over the ruins of a pre-existent Byzantine basilica. Someone has hypothesised that this was the site of the house of the High Priest Caiaphas, but it has not as of yet been confirmed. What has been brought to light meanwhile, is a beautiful street of steps called the maccabean stairs, which in the first century A. D. must have joined Mount Zion to the valley of the Kidron.

The slender, pointed arches of the Coenaculum.

*The exterior of the Church of the ▶
Dormition at sunset and the crypt with the
statue of Mary sleeping.*

Coenaculum - On top of Mount Zion is the Coenaculum, or Room of the Last Supper, where one of the most momentous events in the Christian faith occurred: the institution of the Eucharist. Also, seven weeks later, the Holy Spirit appeared here to Mary and the apostles during the Pentecost. The Crusaders built the present room with its beautiful pointed arches, but in the 15th century, the Moslems took possession of Mount Zion, transforming the church into a mosque and prohib-

iting both Christians and Jews from entering for nearly five centuries.

Church of the Dormition - This is a Benedictine church designed by Heinrich Renard and built at the turn of the century in Romanesque style with a domed bell tower. Here, Mary fell into an «eternal sleep». The church crypt, in fact, contains a statue of Mary, reclining, caught in her final slumber.

The grand sarcophagus of the tomb of David.

General view of the Israel Museum and ▶
the outside of the Shrine of the Book.

Tomb of David - Since the 10th century it has been thought that King David, after his 40-year reign over Israel, was probably buried here, although it is more likely that he was buried on the Ophel with other Israelite kings. A church was built here in the 4th century and was later restored by the Crusaders. In 1524, the Moslems, who venerate El Nabi Daoud as a great prophet, turned this site into a mosque and prohibited Jews and Christians from entering until 1948.

The large stone cenotaph, covered by an ornate cloth featuring the Star of David, has several silver crowns, decorations for the Torah scrolls, symbolizing the kings of Judah who succeeded David.

Israel Museum - Inaugurated in 1965, it was designed by two Israeli architects, Alfred Mansfeld and Dora Gad. It consists of several components whose modern lines fit in perfectly with the surrounding hills, dotted with olive and cypress trees. Its five pavillions are: the Bronfman Biblical and Archaeological Museum, the Bezabel Folk Art exhibit, the Billy Rose Sculpture Gardens, the Ruth Children's Museum and, most important, the *Shrine of the Book* wherein are the Dead Sea Scrolls, the two-thousand year-old biblical manuscripts found in caves at Qumran. The Shrine was designed by the Americans Frederik Kiesler and Armand Bartos. The white dome contrasts with the black basalt wall, symbolizing the envisioned battle between the Sons of Light (the Essenes) and the Sons of Darkness.

◄ *The exterior of the Russian church.*

The interior of the Great Synagogue.

◄ *A suggestive framing of the tomb of Sanhedrin.*

Russian Church - Beautiful green domes topped by golden crosses characterize Jerusalem's Russian-Orthodox church. An enormous stone column 12 yards long lays on the ground in front of it: probably broken off during construction work on the Temple of Herod. During the British mandate of Israel, English authorities occupied part of the convent's apartments transforming them into offices.

Tombs of the Sanhedrin - Also known as the Tombs of the Judges, they are a series of rock catacombs hewn into three separate levels. For the most part, they go back to the 6th century A. D. but some are also from the Maccabean period. Tradition says that members of the Sanhedrin, the Supreme Court and highest religious authority of Temple times, are buried here. The head of the Sanhedrin was the Nasi, or prince, whose position was usually inherited.

Great Synagogue - This is the biggest and most modern synagogue in Israel. Next to it is the synagogue of the Chief Rabbinate of Israel, or Heikhal Shlomo, where Jewish prayer services are held both in the Ashkenazi (European) style and in the Sephardi (North African) style. Inside the synagogue is a beautiful 17th century Ark from Padua, Italy. There is a museum, called Dor va Dor (Generation to Generation), which includes the reconstruction of an old Italian synagogue.

◀ *Close-up, the giant bronze menorah and in the background, the Knesset.*

The famous stained-glass windows by Marc Chagall in the Synagogue of the Hadassah Hospital.

◀ *Exterior of the Convent of the Cross.*

Knesset - The Israeli National Assembly has its headquarters in this building which was inaugurated in 1966. Its construction was financed by James Rothchild and the artists Marc Chagall, Dani Karavan and David Palumbo contributed their works. The Knesset is composed of 120 members who are elected every four years. Facing the main entrance of the building is the large bronze menorah (seven-branched candelabrum), decorated with 29 scenes from the history of Israel. It is the work of the English sculptor Benno Elkian and was a gift of the British Parliament.

Convent of the Cross - Surrounded by a very high wall, the Convent of the Cross rose over a primitive 6th century construction, fortified in its day, — the 11th century, — by Georgians from Caucasus. The tradition says that Lot, escaping the destruction of Sodom, settled here and planted a tree from which the wood was made for the cross of Jesus. Even today, behind the main altar, there is a ring of silver marking the spot where legend says the tree grew.

Hadassah Hospital - Here in Ein Kerem is one of the most beautiful works of art of our day: the stained glass windows by Marc Chagall which were installed and dedicated in the hospital in 1961. The twelve panels, whose colors match those of the breastplate of the High Priest described in the Book of Exodus, represent Jacob's parting words to his twelve sons. These twelve sons were to become most of the twelve tribes of Israel (Joseph was not a tribe, but his two sons, Ephraim and Menashe, were to become half-tribes). With his assistant, Charles Marc, Chagall developed a special technique of using up to three colors in each panel, whereas before, each bit of stained glass had to be isolated by borders of lead.

Yad Vashem - This is a place of commemoration and homage to the six million Jewish victims of the Nazi regime. There are many components of Yad Vashem, including a museum which documents the rise of Hitler's National Socialist Party, the deeds it perpetrated during World War II and the aftermath. Outside there is a towering column dedicated to the memory of all those who resisted Nazism, with the word «Zkor» at the top, Remember. In the Ohel Yizkor, a low building made of unhewn boulders, the visitor will find the names of the major death camps written on the floor. An eternal flame burns next to a vault containing the ashes of some of those who died in the Holocaust.

Rockefeller Museum - Built with funds donated by John D. Rockefeller and designed by English architect Austin Harrison, this museum houses some of the most important archaeological finds in the country. It is an elegant construction of pink and white limestone with an octagonal tower and a courtyard pool around which the exhibit rooms are located.

The sanctuary of Yad Vashem.

The exterior and a room of the ▶
Rockefeller Museum.

A bas-relief in the square of Yad Vashem.

THE GHETTO UPRISING · THE LAST MARCH

Rachel's Tomb - The only one of the biblical matriarchs and patriarchs not buried in Hebron's Machpela Cave, Rachel died in childbirth here on the Bethlehem-Efrat road (Genesis 35:19-20). Her husband, Jacob, placed a marker on the spot. Still today, Rachel's tomb is a favorite site for prayer among Jews, particularly among those who encounter difficulty in bearing children.

BETHLEHEM

A few miles south of Jerusalem along a charming, biblical road, is the hilltop town of Bethlehem. The name Bethlehem has two meanings: in Hebrew, the House of Bread, and in Arabic, the House of Meat.

On both sides of the road are vast, rocky pastures where shepherds tend their flocks of sheep and goats. One of these is aptly called the «Shepherds' Fields» because here the angels announced the birth of Jesus. It was also in these fields that the tender love story between Ruth and Boaz unfolded as narrated in the Book of Ruth. Their son, Obed, was to become the grandfather of King David, who was born in Bethlehem a thousand years before the birth of Jesus. For Christians, Bethlehem is a holy city because

Jesus was born there. «In those days, an edict of Augustus came out for the census of the entire empire.» One of the principal functions of the Roman administration was to impose taxes. Therefore, the census ordered by Augustus, and supervised by the local governor Publius Sulpicius Quirinus, was certain to provide ready monies to the authorities. Since law decreed that every landowner had to declare his property for purposes of taxation, Joseph had to leave Nazareth and return to Bethlehem «...together with his bride, Mary, who was with child. While they were in that place, the moment of birth arrived and there she brought forth her firstborn son, wrapped him in swaddling clothes and laid him in a

Panorama of Bethlehem.

The tiny entrance to the basilica, called the 'door of humility'.

manger because there was no room for them at the inn». This is how the Gospel of Luke describes the event destined to change the history of mankind. The actual birthdate of Jesus is disputed: for Roman Catholics it is December 24, for Greek Orthodox it is January 6 and for the Armenians, January 18. In contempt for the pilgrims who had venerated this place since the earliest times, Emperor Hadrian, in 135 A. D., consecrated the woods and caves here to Adonis and introduced his own pagan cult. In 332, Constantine the Great, after having the woods cut down, ordered the construction of a basilica on the spot. The present structure is a combination of Constantine's basilica (much of which was destroyed two

The interior of the Basilica of the Nativity.

A detail of the silver star that marks ▶
the birthplace of Jesus.

The grotto of the Nativity with the altar ▶
of the birth of Christ and that of the crib.

centuries after its construction), Justin's sixth century renovations and later Crusader repairs. The basilica was miraculously spared during the Persian invasion of 614, because the invaders found a painting of the three Magi, whom they took to be Persians, decorating the pediment.

In 1101, Baldwin I was crowned Crusader king there, and twenty years later, Baldwin II and his wife were, as well. Then came a long decline. In 1646, the Turks melted down the lead from its roof to make cannonballs. About the same time, the Christian community decided to block up the main entrance except for a very small opening, to prevent the locals from riding into the church on horseback. The door is only one and a half yards high, and is sometimes called the «gate of humility» since one has to stoop to enter.

Inside the basilica, red limestone columns with Corinthian capitals line the double aisles on either side of the central nave. Above them, one sees the remnants of mosaics, done in 1169, which have a gold background and depict the ancestors of Jesus and the first seven ecumenical councils. Of these councils, only the first at Constantinopole has survived in its entirety, while fragments of the others, Nicaea, Ephesus and Chalcedon, can also be seen.

The Chapel of the Nativity - This is the small grotto located directly under the main altar of the church. In its small apse a silver star marks the place of Jesus' birth. Above the altar are fifteen lamps belonging to different Christian communities. In a sunken chapel off to the side of the grotto are two altars: the *altar of the crib* where the newborn infant was laid, and the *altar of the Magi*, the three kings who came to worship the newborn king.

The cloister of the Church of St. Catherine, with the statue of St. Jerome.

The interior of the Church of St. Catherine, where Christmas mass is celebrated.

A corner of the cloister of the Church of St. Catherine.

St. Catherine's - Next door to the Church of the Nativity is the Roman Catholic church of St. Catherine. It was built by the Franciscans in 1881 over a cave where, tradition says, St. Jerome lived when he was translating the scriptures from the Greek Septuagint to the Latin Vulgate in the 4th century. A statue of him can be seen in the courtyard, once part of a Crusader cloistered convent, outside. St. Catherine's is where Christmas Midnight Mass is celebrated and relayed throughout the world via satellite.

Panorama of Ein Karem and the interior
of the grotto where John the Baptist
was born.

EIN KAREM

This small village, a western suburb of Jerusalem since 1961, is the biblical Beit Hakerem, «Fountain of the Vineyard». Inhabited by Arabs, it was abandoned in 1948 and resettled by Jewish immigrants in the 1950s. This was the scene of the Visitation, when Mary went to see her cousin Elizabeth, who greeted the future mother of Jesus with the words, «Blessed art thou among women». Mary responded with the «Magnificat», a song of praise to the Lord, inscribed in the Church of the Visitation, built in 1939 by Antonio Barluzzi.

Ein Karem is the birthplace of St. John the Baptist. A fifth-century Franciscan monastery dedicated to him was built on the traditional site of the home of his parents, Elizabeth and Zachary. It was used as a stable by the Arabs but later restored. In the crypt is the **Grotto of Benedictus**, the presumed birthplace of John the Baptist. A marble star in front of the altar recalls the event with these words: «Hic precursor Domini natus est».